HISTORY IN DEPTH

BLACK PEOPLE IN BRITAIN 1650~1850

Tessa Hosking

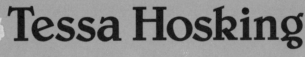

M

Macmillan Education

London and Basingstoke

First published in 1984

Published by
MACMILLAN EDUCATION LIMITED
Houndmills Basingstoke Hampshire RG21 2XS
and London
Associated companies throughout the world

Printed in Hong Kong

British Library Cataloguing in Publication Data
Hosking, Tessa
   Black people in Britain 1650–1850. — (History in depth)
   1. West Indians in Great Britain — History
   I. Title   II. Series
   941′004′969729   DA125.W4

ISBN 0-333-35078-2

CONTENTS

Acknowledgements

The author and publishers wish to acknowledge the following photograph sources:

BBC Hulton Picture Library p 8 bottom; British Library Title page, pp 5, 14, 19, 33 bottom, 40; Dr Johnson's House Trust pp 16, 17; Greater London Council as Trustees of the Iveagh Bequest Kenwood p 25; Guildhall Library p 32; Mansell Collection pp 13 bottom, 22, 23, 28 bottom, 29 bottom, 47; Mary Evans Picture Library p 37; Museum of London p 33 top left; National Galleries of Canada, Ottawa — Sancho p 15; National Galleries of Scotland p 26 top; National Maritime Museum pp 10, 29 top; National Portrait Gallery pp 20, 36; National Trust p 13 top; Paul Mellon Collection, Upperville, Virginia p 26 bottom; By permission of the President and Council of the Royal College of Surgeons of England p 12; Royal Exeter Albert Memorial Museum, Exeter p 42; Surrey Record Office p 28 top; taken from Mayhew — London, Labour and the Poor, Griffin Bohn & Co 1861 p 33 top right.

The author and publishers wish to thank Oxford University Press for permission to reproduce extracts from *Black People in Britain 1555–1833* by F.O. Shyllon (Oxford University Press for the Institute of Race Relations, 1977).

The publishers have made every effort to trace the copyright holders, but if they have inadvertently overlooked any they will be pleased to make the necessary arrangements at the first opportunity.

PREFACE

The study of history is exciting, whether in a good story well told, a mystery solved by the judicious unravelling of clues, or a study of the men, women and children, whose fears and ambitions, successes and tragedies make up the collective memory of mankind.

This series aims to reveal this excitement to pupils through a set of topic books on important historical subjects from the Middle Ages to the present day. Each book contains four main elements: a narrative and descriptive text, lively and relevant illustrations, extracts of contemporary evidence, and questions for further thought and work. Involvement in these elements should provide an adventure which will bring the past to life in the imagination of the pupil.

Each book is also designed to develop the knowledge, skills and concepts so essential to a pupil's growth. It provides a wide, varying introduction to the evidence available on each topic. In handling this evidence, pupils will increase their understanding of basic historical concepts like causation and change, as well as of more advanced ideas like revolution and democracy. In addition, their use of basic study skills will be complemented by more sophisticated historical skills such as the detection of bias and the formulation of opinion.

The intended audience for the series is pupils of eleven to sixteen years: it is expected that the earlier topics will be introduced in the first three years of secondary school, while the nineteenth and twentieth century topics are directed towards first examinations.

SLAVES IN BRITAIN

> To be SOLD,
>
> A Black Girl, the Property of John Bull, Eleven Years of Age, who is extremely handy, works at her Needle tolerably, and speaks English perfectly well; is of an excellent Temper, and willing Disposition.
>
> Enquire of Mrs. Owen, at the Angel Inn, behind St. Clement's Church in the Strand.

Advertisement from the Public Ledger

To be sold, a Negro Boy, about fourteen years old, . . . has been used two years to all kinds of household work, and to wait at table; his price is £25, and would not be sold but the person he belongs to is leaving off business. Apply at the bar of George Coffee-house in Chancery Lane, over against the Gate.

Advertisement in the *London Advertiser*, 1756

These advertisements are typical of many which appeared in British newspapers throughout the late seventeenth and eighteenth centuries, and as such provide us with the clearest of evidence that black people were at that time regarded by many British people as property which could be bought and sold. People who are regarded as property are generally called slaves, but it was never clear whether that term was legally accurate in Britain before 1834. Slavery was finally abolished throughout the British Empire in 1834, but before that time enough people thought that slavery was legal in Britain for many thousands of black people to be kept and treated as slaves, from as early as the sixteenth century.

Some black people were brought to Britain to be sold as slaves straight away, as we can tell from other examples of advertisements and announcements in newspapers. In the *Liverpool Chronicle*, for instance, an auctioneer called James Parker announced that he had for sale: 'a fine negro boy 11 years of age, imported from Bonny, by Mr Thomas Yates, a Guinea merchant'; and an issue of the *Bristol Intelligence* advertised for sale: 'a Negro Boy, a lad of 14 years, recently landed'. Bristol and Liverpool were the two chief slave-

Bonny: a town on the coast of present day Nigeria

trading ports in Britain, and many such sales took place in them. On 12 September 1766 *Williamson's Liverpool Advertiser* offered no fewer than: 'eleven negroes' for sale, adding that they had been 'imported ... [by] the *Angola*' and that they were 'to be sold at the Exchange Coffee-house in Water Street ... at one o'clock precisely'.

Another way that black people came to be sold was when their 'owners' died. In 1763, for instance, a man named John Rice was hanged for forgery at Tyburn. Reporting on the sale of his property after his execution, *The Gentleman's Magazine* announced that:

> *At the sale of Rice the broker's effects, a Negro boy was put up by Auction, and sold for £32.*

Black people were also sometimes bequeathed in wills. In October 1718, for instance, a merchant named Becher Fleming left 'my negro boy, named Tallow' to Mrs Mary Becher. And in 1715 a sea-captain called Nightingale bequeathed 'the proceeds of his two boys and girls, then on board his ship'.

It is impossible now to know how many white British people were shocked by instances such as these, or how many took them for granted or did not care, but newspaper reports occasionally expressed disapproval. In 1771, for instance, *The Stamford Mercury* reported that:

> *At a sale of a gentleman's effects at Richmond, a Negro Boy was put up and sold for £32 ... a shocking instance in a free country.*

But how did black people themselves react to being regarded and treated as slaves? Many rebelled in the most direct way possible – by running away from their 'owners'. We have evidence of this in the advertisements for their return which appeared in newspapers:

> *Negro 22 years – run away – middle Size, with English stammering speech; cut on forehead; Jerusalem Arms, West Indies, 1706 [branded] on Left Arm; 1 guinea for Return, or voluntary Pardon.*
> Advertisement in the *Daily Courant*, March 1712

The following examples show us that one young black man, called Toby, was determined not to accept slavery in Britain:

> *Black Boy named Toby, aged about 19, being pretty tall and slender, and his Hair newly cut off; he wore a blue Livery with Brass Buttons lined with Orange colour, and was seen in Essex the day he went away.*

> *Toby a Black Boy, aged about 19, pretty Tall and Slender, his Hair cut short; servant to William Johnson Esq.; of Bromley in Middlesex, made his escape last Tuesday Morning....*
> Advertisements placed by William Johnson in *The London Gazette*, 23–26 March and 7–11 May 1691

Many other black people brought to Britain as slaves did not make their bid for freedom by running away, but nevertheless made it clear to their 'owners' that they were unwilling any longer to be treated as slaves. A writer in *The Gentleman's Magazine* of October 1764 complained that:

> *Negroe servants (imported) into these kingdoms ... cease to consider themselves as slaves in this free country, nor will they put up with inequality of treatment, nor more willingly perform the labourious offices of servitude than our own people, and if put to it, are generally sullen ... and revengeful.*

servitude: slavery

The writer Sir John Fielding complained that black people brought:

> *... to England as cheap servants having no right to wages ... no sooner arrive here than they put themselves on a footing with other servants ... and ... begin to expect wages according to their own opinion of their merits....*
>
> Sir John Fielding, *Penal Laws*, 1768

Questions
(These questions could all be used for discussion).

1 Most of the black people mentioned in the evidence are young and male. Can you think of a reason for this?

2 a What did the *Stamford Mercury* call, in 1771, 'a shocking instance in a free country'?

   b Why do you think that it described it as 'shocking'?

   c Do you think that it was shocking? Give a reason for your answer.

3 Considering the evidence presented in this chapter, what reasons would you say black people in Britain had for running away from their 'owners'?

4 a Judging by the remarks made by the last two writers quoted, how did those who did not run away show that they would no longer 'consider themselves as slaves'?

   b Why, do you think, did these two writers resent this?

   c Why, in particular, did Sir John Fielding consider that black people brought to England had 'no right to wages'?

   d Why, do you think, did the black people themselves consider that they *had* a right to them?

   e Do *you* consider that they had a right to them? Give reasons for your answer.

2 BLACK PEOPLE IN BRITAIN

Queen Elizabeth I

... there are of late divers blackamores brought into this realm, of which kind of people there are already here to manie, consideryng howe God hath blessed this land with great increase of people of our own nation ... those kinde of people should be sente forth of the land....

Letter from Queen Elizabeth I to the lord mayors of England's major cities, 1596

In 1601, five years after this letter, a Royal Proclamation was issued, making even clearer Queen Elizabeth I's instructions that all black people ('blackamores') then in England should be repatriated. There is no evidence, however, that these instructions were followed, and this is perhaps hardly surprising since the Queen herself employed black people at court, as had her father, Henry VIII, and as did her royal successors. Indeed, the fashion of keeping black servants, which began in the sixteenth century, lasted right into the nineteenth century, and was copied by a growing number of people during the seventeenth and eighteenth centuries.

Why, though, had these early black residents of Britain come here? For an answer to this question we must turn our attention first of all to the European colonies which had grown up in South America and the Caribbean islands following the Spanish conquest of those areas in the late fifteenth and early sixteenth centuries. The early Spanish settlers in these colonies found that they were short of labour to work their land, and decided that the answer to their problem was to import African people as slaves. As early as 1518, an official in the island of Hispaniola asked that: 'permission be given to bring in Negroes, a race robust for labour'.

The west coast of Africa had, since the late fifteenth century, been claimed by the Portuguese, who therefore regarded it as their right and privilege to supply the Spanish colonists with slaves. A number of Englishmen, however, soon saw that there was money to be made by breaking into this trade, and they were supported in their attempts to do so by Elizabeth I herself. One of the first and most successful of these English slave-traders was Sir John Hawkins, who can be said to have started the Triangular Trade with his voyage of 1562.

The diagram shows how the Triangular Trade worked. As you can see, African people, taken and then sold as slaves, formed its most profitable part. Not only did they create profit through being bought and sold, but they were the labour which produced the goods which made profit on the final stage. Most of the profit – and therefore

Charles I, his family and others on the river at Hampton Court. Notice his black servant

The Triangular Trade *operated in three stages, at each of which a profit was made:*

1 Ships sailed from Britain with manufactured goods such as cloth, iron, guns and brandy which were exchanged on the west coast of Africa for slaves
2 The slaves were taken on the 'middle passage' to the West Indies and North and South America, where they were sold to provide labour for the plantations
3 The ships returned to Britain laden with the luxuries and raw materials (sugar, cotton, tobacco, rum) which had been produced by slave labour

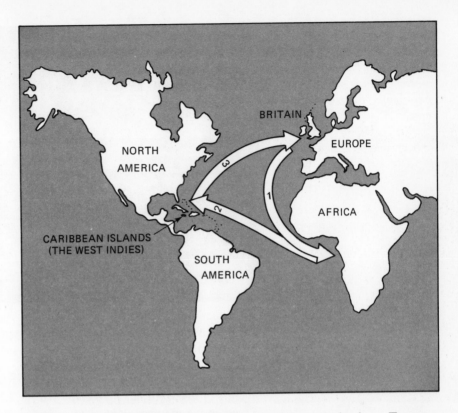

wealth – from the Triangular Trade found its way back to Europe, and most of this found its way to Britain. Indeed, without this wealth, Britain would not have been able to make such rapid progress with the Industrial Revolution.

The cities which benefited most from the Triangular Trade were the sea-ports of London, Bristol and Liverpool, from which the slave ships sailed and whose merchants became some of the richest people in the land. It is not surprising therefore, that most of the black people in Britain lived in these cities.

At first they came mainly as slaves in the possession of the captains of ships returning from a voyage. Slave-captains would keep a few slaves for themselves as a sort of bonus, and sell them in England before they went off on another voyage.

Writing about Bristol in the eighteenth century, a nineteenth-century writer has given us this description of the captains of slave ships:

> *... they were accustomed to flaunt large silver, and sometimes gold, buttons on their apparel, and their shoes were decorated with buckles of the precious metals. But the most distinguishing mark of a captain in the streets was the black slave who attended him, and who was often sold to a wealthy family when the owners again embarked for Africa.*

> J. Latimer, *Annals of Bristol in the Eighteenth Century*, Bristol, 1893

Captain Lord George Graham and his friends in his cabin in 1745. The captain's black slave is entertaining them with music.
Can you tell what instruments he is playing?

The following is an example of the type of advertisement which appeared frequently in newspapers:

> *For sale immediately, ONE stout NEGRO young fellow, about 20 years of age, that has been employed for 12 months on board a ship, and is a very serviceable hand. And a NEGRO BOY, about 12 years old, that has been used since Sept. last to wait at table, and is of a very good disposition, both warranted sound. Apply to Robert Williamson, Broker. N.B. A vessel from 150 to 250 tons burthen is wanted to be purchased.*
>
> *Williamson's Liverpool Advertiser, 24 June 1757*

Questions
1 How would you describe Queen Elizabeth I's attitude towards black people?
2 a On what sort of person's behalf do you think that the 'Broker' placed the advertisement of 24 June 1757 in *Williamson's Liverpool Advertiser*? How can you tell?
  b Why might the evidence provided by this advertisement be more trustworthy than that provided by the extract just before it?

Because it was at first so rare to have a black slave as a servant, the possession of one must have excited curiosity and envy amongst a person's friends and acquaintances. This in turn led to more black people being imported as slaves, and so the number of black people in Britain grew. (Another attraction of keeping slaves instead of ordinary servants, of course, was that slaves did not have to be paid wages.)

Meanwhile, the English, along with the French and the Dutch, were taking over from the Spanish as colonisers in the West Indies (as the Caribbean islands came to be called). The English settlers were determined to make a success of agriculture there, and the first crop which they tried successfully was tobacco. To grow it they used the labour of poor Englishmen who were bound to work for them for a period of five or ten years. Then, about the middle of the seventeenth century, sugar was tried, and proved to be a very successful crop. To be as profitable as possible, however, sugar had to be grown on a very large scale – on large plantations, using a very large workforce. The settlers could see only one way of getting the large workforce they needed and still make a profit, and that was by using slave labour from Africa. Thus, from the middle of the seventeenth century, the trade in slaves from Africa – via the Triangular Trade – increased enormously. By 1770, more than 100 000 people a year were being taken from Africa to slavery in the 'New World'.

New World: America including the Caribbean islands

The success of the sugar industry in the West Indies meant, of course, that the West Indian planters (as those who owned the plantations were called) became very prosperous indeed. And it was they who were largely responsible for the now even greater increase in the number of black people who came to live in Britain. For when they returned home to Britain, either for good or just for a holiday, planter families would bring with them large numbers of their black slaves as domestic servants. This was sneered at by some people as 'show and extravagance', but it was also envied by many, so that the demand for black servants grew once more. Planter families who wished to sell their black slaves in Britain in order to save on fares when they returned to the West Indies had no difficulty in doing so.

It was not just slave-ship captains and West Indian planters, however, who brought black people to England as slaves. Others who did so included ordinary sailors, officials returning from overseas service in the British Empire, English gentlemen returning from private travels abroad, and even King George I who, when he arrived in 1714 to take his place on the throne, brought with him two black Mohammedan body-servants named Mustapha and Mahomet, to attend to his personal needs.

Furthermore, even before the end of the seventeenth century, some Africans were being brought directly from their homelands (rather than via the West Indies or America) to be sold in Britain.

However, not all black people in Britain were African or of African origin. During the eighteenth century, for instance, numbers of Indian domestic servants were brought back to Britain by officials of the East India Company.

Nor did all black people who came to Britain come as slaves. Some came as free sailors on British ships. Some came as free men or women from the West Indies. And quite a number came from Africa as students. Indeed, the first record we have of Africans being brought to

11

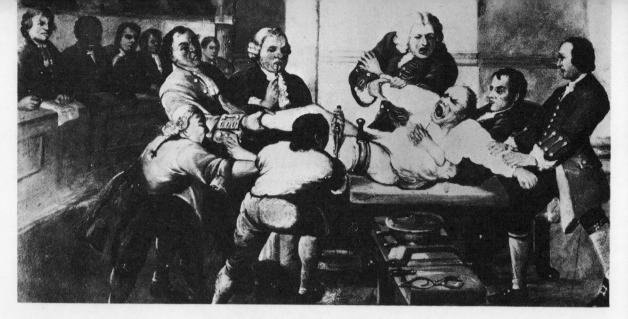

An eighteenth century amputation scene. Notice the black medical student among those watching

Britain is of five who were brought by the English trader John Lok, so that they could learn English, and then return to Africa where they would 'be a help to Englishmen' as interpreters. This was in 1555.

African kings and chiefs were often very keen to send their sons to be educated in Europe, but it was also in the interests of the European trading companies:

> *It has always been the practice of merchants and commanders of ships to Africa, to encourage the natives to send their children to England; as it not only conciliates their friendship, and softens their manners, but adds greatly to the security of the traders.*
>
> *Memoirs of the late Captain Hugh Crow of Liverpool*, 1830

It was, however, the prosperity of the West Indian colonies from the middle of the seventeenth to the end of the eighteenth centuries – a prosperity based on slavery – which, more than anything else, resulted in black people being brought to Britain, and so led to the large black population which existed in Britain during this same period.

Questions

3 a What do you think Captain Crow meant when he wrote that the sending of African children to England 'adds greatly to the security of the traders'?

   b Do you think that African kings and chiefs were wise to send their children to Europe to be educated? Give as many reasons for your answer as you can.

4 List the reasons given in this chapter for black people living in Britain in the seventeenth, eighteenth and nineteenth centuries; then consider how important each of these reasons is, and list them in order of importance.

3

MENSERVANTS

A very wide range of people – from all but the poorest ranks in society – were able to keep at least one servant in the seventeenth and eighteenth centuries. Thus black people brought to this country found themselves as servants to people ranging from small shopkeepers to the wealthiest lords and ladies.

As we saw in the last chapter, the reasons for white people keeping black people as servants in Britain varied, but among the very wealthy – and those who wished to copy them – it became the fashionable thing to do. This perhaps explains why black men were often employed as coachmen and footmen, for these servants were kept largely for show.

A postilion at Erddig Park, Flintshire, in the mid-eighteenth century. A postilion rode one of the horses that drew the coach, to guide the team of horses if a coachman was not driving

There were about as many ranks within the servant class as there were in society as a whole, the highest-ranking servants living quite comfortable lives, and indeed being waited on by the lower servants, some of whom worked very long and hard hours for very little pay. The lower menservants mostly wore livery, i.e. uniforms.

The main menservants, in order of rank:

Upper servants	*Servants in livery*
Land steward	Coachman
House steward	Footman
Man-cook	Groom
Bailiff	Porter
Valet or personal servant	Gamekeeper
Butler	Postilion
Gardener	Footboy

Illustration from Vanity Fair showing a black footman. The appearance of black servants in this novel, which first appeared in 1847, shows that they were employed well into the nineteenth century

As we saw in chapter 1, black servants were often still regarded as slaves. However, those who, by the second half of the eighteenth century, were advertising their services in newspapers must certainly have been free. They were, moreover, usually seeking fairly high-ranking servant positions:

AS VALET OR UPPER FOOTMAN with a Single Gentleman, or in a Family, a genteel Young Man, a Black, who can shave well, and dress hair in the present taste; has been in that capacity in England many years, and can have an undeniable character from his last place. Please to direct for S.J. No. 7, Gerrard-Street, Soho.
Advertisement in *The World*, 6 February 1788

AS VALET to a Single Gentleman, or SERVANT in a genteel family, either for a constancy or for a season, a Black Young Man, a native of Africa, who has been mostly brought up in London; can dress hair incomparably well, and is qualified for the duty of a Servant; is of an active and affable disposition. Direct for J. A. at No. 5, Charles-street, near Baker-street, Portman-square.

Questions

1 Using the table showing *The main menservants, in order of rank*, list the black menservants shown in the pictures on page 13 in order of rank. Are either, or both of them wearing livery?

2 How can we tell that the servants who advertised their services in newspapers were free?

3 Do you think that the two men who advertised in *The World* in the advertisements shown here would have got the positions they were seeking? Give reasons for your answer.

There were a few black men who attained almost the highest ranks of the domestic servant class. The three that we shall look at next, all worked as personal servants, although the men whom they served, and the lives that they led, differed widely. The first of these was Ignatius Sancho. His start in life could not have been less favourable, for he was born aboard a slave ship, of African parents who died shortly afterwards. Brought to Britain at the age of two, he spent the years of his youth in the service of three unmarried ladies in Greenwich. He wrote of this time later:

The first part of my life was rather unlucky, as I was placed in a family who judged ignorance the best and only security for obedience. — A little reading and writing I got by unwearied application. — The latter part of my life has been – thro' God's blessing, truly fortunate, having spent it in the service of one of the best families in the Kingdom.

Letter to Lawrence Sterne, July 1766

The second family Sancho referred to was the Montagu family, with whom he had become acquainted accidentally:

The late Duke of Montagu lived on Blackheath: he accidentally saw the little Negro, and admired in him a native frankness of manner as yet unbroken by servitude, and unrefined by education — He brought him frequently home to the Duchess, (and) indulged his turn for reading with presents of books....

Memoirs of his Life by Joseph Jekyll, MP, prefixed to the
Letters of the late Ignatius Sancho

Not until he was about twenty, however, did Sancho, in whom 'the love of freedom had increased with years', leave the three ladies, who were strict and unpleasant:

His noble patron (the Duke) was recently dead. — Ignatius flew to the Duchess for protection.... The Duchess secretly admired his character; and at length consented to admit him into her household, where he remained as butler till her death, when he found himself, by her Grace's bequest and his own economy, possessed of seventy pounds in money, and an annuity of thirty.

Memoirs of his Life

After a short while spent enjoying 'freedom, riches, and leisure', Sancho 'turned his mind once more to service ... and the present Duke soon placed him about his person'. As valet, or personal servant, to the new Duke, he was even more highly placed in the servant hierarchy than he had been as butler. The following extracts from a letter he wrote while on holiday, in Dalkeith, Scotland, with the family in 1770, give us a good impression of the pleasant lifestyle enjoyed by many upper servants:

the freedom of Dumbarton: to be given the 'freedom' of a city is to be officially made one of its citizens, and is regarded as an honour

We came home from our Highland excursion last Monday night, safe and well – after escaping manifold dangers. — Mesdames H —, D, and self, went in the post-coach, and were honor'd with the freedom of Dumbarton.... Inverary is a charming place.... We had herrings in perfection – and would have had mackerel; but the scoundrels were too sharp for us – and would not be caught.... We paraded to Edinburgh last Friday in a post coach and four: H —, D, Mrs M —, housekeeper, and self were the party; — we saw the usual seeings, and dined at Lord Chief Baron's....

... I hear nothing of moving as yet – pray God speed us southward! though we have fine weather – fine beef – fine ale – and fine ladies. Lady Mary grows a little angel; the Duchess gets pretty round – they all eat – drink – and seem pure merry ... farewell.

Letter IX, Letters of the late Ignatius Sancho

Ignatius Sancho had to retire from service due to ill-health:

Towards the close of the year 1773, repeated attacks of the gout, and a constitutional corpulence, rendered him incapable of further attendance in the Duke's family.

Memoirs of his Life

Ignatius Sancho in 1768

We shall see what he did after this in chapter 6.

Jack Beef was another black personal manservant. He was, in many respects, treated very favourably, but unlike Ignatius Sancho he remained a slave almost to his dying day. We know about his life from the diary kept by his master, John Baker, who had been Solicitor-General of the Leeward Islands in the West Indies. We learn from this that he attended his master on horseback, went on important messages for him in London, and was much in demand among his friends for cooking turtles and bottling wines! He went out fox-hunting when in the country and, when in London, accompanied the other (mainly white) servants to the theatre, as well as attending dances organised by the black community there. When, after many years of faithful service, Jack Beef was declared a free man, he decided to leave his master and England, and return with his small savings to the West Indies. This, though, was not to be, for he died four days later, apparently after a short illness:

Jan.7. 1771. Jack Beef died yesterday after a good dinner, when he said he was better and would take a nap on bed; he did so and seemed to sleep quiet, but went and died in his sleep.

The Diary of John Baker

The funeral of Jack Beef took place on 10 January 1771, attended by at least one of his relatives, the Baker family, and his fellow servants.

The third personal servant we shall look at is Francis Barber, who worked for the famous writer Dr Samuel Johnson for nearly thirty years. Johnson treated his black servant as an equal member of his household, for very deliberate reasons: he wanted to demonstrate to the world his antipathy to slavery and the slave trade, and many, such as his biographer James Boswell, were shocked by his principles.

When he died Johnson left all his papers and personal belongings to Francis, including £70 a year to live on, which was then far more than a nobleman would have considered necessary to leave to a faithful servant.

Francis Barber had become Samuel Johnson's servant in 1752, at the age of about ten, just after Johnson's wife and Francis's previous master had died. The latter, Colonel Bathurst, who had brought Francis to England from Jamaica in 1750, had granted the boy his freedom in his will and left him £12. He had also had him baptised, and sent him to school.

Some fifteen years later, Johnson decided to send Francis to school again. So in 1767 (at the age of twenty-five!) Francis went to Bishops Stortford Grammar School in Hertfordshire, where he remained for about five years. During this time Johnson wrote him several letters, three of which he kept and was able to give to Boswell to include in *The Life of Johnson*. The following extracts from these tell us something about the relationship which must have existed between Johnson and Francis Barber:

Francis Barber

A Literary Party at Sir Joshua Reynolds, *by James E. Doyle. The black servant here may be Francis Barber, who is known to have waited at the table of Sir Joshua Reynolds. Reynolds was a portrait painter, and a close friend of Dr. Johnson*

May 28, 1768.
Dear Francis,

. . . I am glad to hear that you are well, and design to come soon to see you. I would have you stay at Mrs. Clapp's for the present, till I can determine what we shall do. Be a good boy. . .

I am, Yours affectionately,
Sam. Johnson.

London, Sep. 25, 1770.
Dear Francis,

. . . I am very well satisfied with your progress, if you can really perform the exercises which you are set. . .

Let me know what English books you read for your entertainment. You can never be wise unless you love reading.

Do not imagine that I shall forget or forsake you; for if, when I examine you, I find that you have not lost [wasted] your time, you shall want no encouragement from. . .

Yours affectionately,
Sam. Johnson

Dec.7. 1770
Dear Francis,

I hope you mind your business. I design you shall stay with Mrs Clapp these holidays. If you are invited out you may go, if Mr. Ellis gives leave. I have ordered you some clothes, which you will receive, I believe, next week. . .

I am Your affectionate,
Sam. Johnson

17

His spell at school was the third time that Francis had left Johnson, for he had twice before left of his own accord. On the first occasion, in 1756, he went to work in an apothecary's (chemist's) shop, in Cheapside. Whilst there, he visited Johnson regularly. On the second occasion, however, he 'ran away to sea'. This must have seemed a particular act of defiance to Johnson, who was well known to 'rail against ships and sailors', saying that 'Being in a ship is [like] being in a jail, with the chance of being drowned'. We do not know why Francis decided to join the Navy as a clerical officer, but since he was not physically strong, and suffered from bronchitis, it was probably lucky for him that Johnson had him sent home after two years.

It was also lucky for a young English woman called Elizabeth, for she had fallen in love with him before he left. Eventually Francis married Betsy, as he called her, and she too joined Johnson's small household. This household was a strange one, being made up of an odd assortment of friends and servants. Francis's duties in it were the usual ones for a personal manservant, of fetching coffee and clothes, booking rooms when they travelled, and waiting on him and his friends at table. It is a touching detail that Johnson himself collected oysters for the cat, rather than ask Francis to wait on an animal.

When Dr Johnson died in 1784, Francis moved with his wife and family to Lichfield, as Johnson had advised him to do, and was there often visited by Johnson's old friends and acquaintances. In 1793 a reporter from *The Gentleman's Magazine* met him, and wrote of him:

Francis is low of stature, marked with the smallpox, has lost his teeth; appears aged and infirm; clean and neat. He spends his time fishing, cultivating a few potatoes, and a little reading.

A few years later the family moved to the village of Burntwood, where Francis and his wife ran a small school. His health got steadily worse, however, and in January 1801 he was taken to hospital. There, in the Stafford Infirmary, he had 'a painful operation', but died soon after it. He was buried in St Mary's Churchyard, Stafford, on 28 January 1801.

It was not just in England that black menservants were to be found. Some also lived in Scotland and Wales, often on the large estates of wealthy families. We know of one who lived in the highlands of Scotland: James Boswell records meeting him while on a tour to the Hebrides with Dr Johnson in 1773. The man was called Gory, and was the servant of Lord Monboddo, whom they visited:

Gory ... was sent as our guide so far. I observed how curious it was to see an African in the north of Scotland, with little or no difference of manners ... (Johnson) laughed to see Gory and Joseph (Boswell's servant): 'Those two fellows, one from Africa, the other from Bohemia – quite at home.' ... When Gory was going to leave us, Mr Johnson called to him, 'Mr. Gory, give me leave to ask you a

John Ystumllyn

question. Are you baptized?' Gory told him he was – and confirmed by the Bishop of Durham.

James Boswell, *Journal of a Tour to the Hebrides with Samuel Johnson*

This is all we know now about Gory, but we know a little more about John Ystumllyn, who lived most of his life in Wales. He had been kidnapped in West Africa around 1750, by a Welshman who took him back to his home in Wales. There he was taught both English and Welsh 'by the ladies of the family', and later worked as a gardener. In 1768 he married Margaret, one of the maidservants, at Dolgellau church, his best man being Gruffydd Williams, the son of a local vicar. Some time after this he was appointed as steward at a nearby mansionhouse and he and his wife brought up a large family there.

Questions

4   In what important way or ways did the life of Jack Beef differ from that of Ignatius Sancho's? Consider in particular the differences in the relationship which each man had with his employer or master.
5   a   How would you describe the relationship which existed between Francis Barber and Dr Johnson?
    b   What pieces of evidence tell us most about this relationship?
    c   Why, do you think, did Francis Barber run away to sea? Do you think, for instance, that the reason had more to do with his relationship with Johnson, or with his feelings about living in Britain in general?
6   Explain, in your own words, what we learn about Gory from the short entry about him in James Boswell's *Journal of a Tour to the Hebrides*.
7   Referring again to the table showing the rank of menservants, say which manservant described in this chapter attained the highest servant position.

4

WOMEN SERVANTS

5th April 1669. For a cookmaid we have, ever since Bridget went, used a black a moor of Mr. Bataliers's [called] Doll, who dresses our meat mighty well, and we mightily pleased with her.

Entry in the Diary of Samuel Pepys

As this entry in the famous diary of Samuel Pepys shows us, black women were employed as domestic servants in British households at least from the middle of the seventeenth century. They were not, however, kept for show in the same way that many black menservants were, for women servants in general were kept for the most part to carry out the behind-the-scenes work of the household. This may partly explain why there were never so many black women servants in Britain as black menservants.

There were fewer upper servant positions for women than there were for men, and women servants were generally regarded as lower in rank than menservants (and were paid less) even when they performed similar duties.

The main women servants, in order of rank:

Upper servants	Lower servants
Lady's maid	Chambermaid
Housekeeper	Housemaid
Cook	Maid of all work
	Laundry maid/dairy maid
	Scullery maid

Portrait of the Duchess of Portsmouth and her black girl servant, 1682
Explain how the artist has used the presence of the black girl to draw attention to (i) the fashionable beauty and (ii) the wealth of the white lady

Most of the evidence we have about black women servants is small and scattered. In *The Daily Advertiser* of 26 April 1765, for example, we find a young black woman advertising for a place as a laundry maid in a gentleman's family. And the will of William Rudd, dated 1741, tells us that he left to Sabina, his black maid, a cottage, an allowance of £5 a year, and half his household goods, in return for years of loyal service.

Two black women servants about whom we know more, however, are Mary Prince and Dido Elizabeth Lindsay, and they provide us with two very different cases.

Mary Prince was brought from Antigua by Mr and Mrs Wood in 1828. In 1831 *The History of Mary Prince, A West Indian Slave, Related by Herself* was published in London. In this extract from it Mary, who suffered from rheumatism, tells what happened one day when she decided to stand up to her mistress:

I told her I was too ill to wash such heavy things that day. She said, she supposed I thought myself a free woman (in England) but I was not; and if I did not do it directly I should be instantly turned out of doors ... I did not know well what to do. I ... did not know where to go ... and therefore, I did not like to leave the house ... at last I took courage and resolved that I would not be longer thus treated.... This was the fourth time they had threatened to turn me out, and, go where I might, I was determined now to take them at their word; though I thought it very hard, after I had lived with them for thirteen years, and worked for them like a horse, to be driven out in this way, like a beggar.

Dido Elizabeth Lindsay was the illegitimate daughter of an African woman, whose name we do not know, and Sir John Lindsay. (Sir John was the nephew of Lord Mansfield, the judge in the case of James Somerset, a black man who was claiming his freedom, which we shall look at in chapter 8.) This is how she came to be born in England:

Sir John Lindsay having taken her mother prisoner in a Spanish vessel, brought her to England, where she was delivered of this girl, of which she was then with child, and which was taken care of by Lord Mansfield, and has been educated by his family.
    Peter Hutchinson, ed. *The Diary and Letters of His Excellency Thomas Hutchinson Esq.* Boston, 1884–6

Unfortunately we do not know what happened to Dido Elizabeth's mother, but the fact that Sir John Lindsay was her father was made clear in the obituary notice which appeared after his death:

Mulatto: person with one black and one white parent

Sir John Lindsay ... has died ... without any legitimate issue, but has left one natural daughter, a Mulatto, who has been brought up in Lord Mansfield's family almost from her infancy.
    The Morning Herald and The London Chronicle, 9 Jan 1788

Dido Elizabeth's position in Lord Mansfield's family, once she had grown up, seems to have been that of an important servant. According to Thomas Hutchinson, who visited the family in 1779:

She is a sort of Superintendent over the dairy, poultry yard, etc.; which we visited, and she was called upon by my Lord every minute for this and that, and showed the greatest attention to everything he said.

She seems to have been very favoured as a servant, for Hutchinson recorded in his diary that she:

... came in after dinner and sat with the ladies, and after coffee, walked with the company in the gardens, one of the young ladies having her arm within the other.

Playing cards at a party. Could one of the ladies pictured be Dido Elizabeth Lindsay? Give at least two reasons for your answer

According to Sir John's obituary notice, Dido Elizabeth was both clever and friendly, and was held in 'the highest respect' by all of Lord Mansfield's relations and visitors.

Despite all this, however, Lord Mansfield felt it necessary to state in his will (dated 17 April 1783) that Dido Elizabeth was a free person. He also left her £100 a year for life, and £500 in money, which would then have allowed her to live very comfortably. Sir John Lindsay, in his will, left her about £500 in trust.

Questions

1 a What part of the evidence regarding Dido Elizabeth Lindsay tells us that slavery still existed in Britain in the last quarter of the eighteenth century?

   b What part of the evidence regarding Mary Prince tells us that slavery still existed in Britain during the first half of the nineteenth century?

2 This chapter suggests two reasons why we do not have as much evidence about black women servants as about black menservants. What are they? Can you think of any others?

3 a Evidence is presented in this chapter about six women or girl servants. List these six, giving their names where possible. Then, next to each, describe the *type* of evidence we have about her, e.g. diary entry, advertisement, picture.

   b Do you think that any of the pieces of evidence are more – or less – reliable than others? Consider, for example:
   Who wrote, or painted the evidence.
   Why that person wrote, or painted it.
   Whether it was written at the time referred to, or later.

5

BOY SERVANTS

shock dog: shaggy-haired
poodle
turbant: turban

Sir,

I am a six year-old blackmoor boy, and have, by my lady's order, been christened by the chaplain. The good man has gone further with me, and told me a great deal of news; as that I am as good as my lady herself, as I am a Christian, and many other things; but for all this, the parrot who came with me from our country is as much esteemed by her as I am. Besides this, the shock dog has a collar that cost as much as mine. I desire also to know whether, now I am Christian, I am obliged to dress like a Turk and wear a turbant. I am, sir, your most obedient servant,

Pompey.

Letter published in *The Tatler*, November 1710

Plate 2 of A Harlot's Progress *and (below)* Taste in High Life. *These cartoons by William Hogarth show the ways in which young black boys were often regarded by fashionable ladies of the period. While the lady in* Taste in High Life *clearly regards the little boy as some sort of pet, the less well-off woman in* A Harlot's Progress *keeps a black boy as an attendant in order to appear fashionable*

We do not know whether the letter was actually written by a six-year-old boy called Pompey, or whether Richard Steele, the owner of the magazine, had made it up in order to draw attention to the practice highlighted by William Hogarth in his famous cartoons (see previous page). This was the practice, which had become very fashionable among ladies by the eighteenth century, of keeping a young black boy as a servant, but almost, in their eyes, as a kind of pet. Such boys became known at the time as 'little black boys', and were often given classical names such as Pompey or Socrates.

It was quite normal for a lady to have a page (a young boy servant who was more privileged than the other servants) but there were a number of ways in which the position of the 'little black boy' was different. For a start, the lady would probably consider that she owned him, rather than that she employed him. In other words, he was a slave. He might even have been 'given' to her as a present:

Dear Mama,

George Hanger has sent me a Black boy, eleven years old and very honest, but the Duke don't like me having a black, yet I cannot bear the poor wretch being ill-used; if you liked him instead of Michel I will send him, he will be a cheap servant and you will make a Christian of him and a good boy; if you don't like him they say Lady Rockingham wants one.

Letter written by the Duchess of Devonshire to her mother in the late eighteenth century

It was common even to rivet a silver or copper collar around the neck of black boys who were kept as slaves. One reason for this can be seen from the following advertisement, which appeared in *The London Gazette* in 1688:

A black boy, an Indian, about thirteen years old, run away the 8th ... from Putney, with a collar about his neck with this inscription: 'The Lady Bromfield's black, in Lincoln's Inn Fields.' Whoever brings him to Sir Edward Bromfield's at Putney, shall have a guinea reward.

Looking back over a hundred years later, the writer Charles Dickens tells us that it was the duty of the 'little black boy' to attend his mistress's person and tea-table, to carry her train as she moved to and fro, to take charge of her fan and smelling-salts, to feed her parrots, and to comb her lap dogs. In the opinion of many people even at the time, however, he was kept more for show than for work. He was dressed in extremely lavish costume, which was often oriental in appearance. He also had to be good-looking, as we can see:

Wanted immediately a Black boy. He must be of a deep black complexion, and a lively, humane disposition, with good features, and not above 15, nor under 12 years of age.

Advertisement in a Liverpool newspaper, 20 August 1756

What happened to these black boys when they grew up? Many became liveried or upper menservants in the same household where they had grown up. The story of one boy, however, has a tragic ending. He was kept as a treasured possession by the Duchess of Kingston from about five years old. She dressed him in great style and took him everywhere with her, including to the theatre. As he grew older, however, he was treated with less favour. He had, for instance, to ride outside her coach instead of inside it. In his teens she sent him to school, but he was apparently lazy there and started mixing with bad company and staying out all night. In the end, the Duchess of Kingston packed him off to the West Indies – and slavery.

Henrietta of Lorraine by Van Dyck.
This seventeenth century Dutch picture of a lady and her 'little black boy' shows that it was fashionable to have black servants in other European countries as well as Britain

Questions

1   a   Describe how the boys in Hogarth's cartoons are dressed.
    b   Why do you think it was so fashionable to dress 'little black boys' in oriental costume?

2   How did a lady's 'little black boy' help her to show off: (a) her wealth; (b) her beauty (the picture of *Henrietta* of *Lorraine* may help you to answer this).

3   a   Why does the Duchess of Devonshire say to her mother that her black boy 'will be a cheap servant' for her?
    b   What does the Duchess of Devonshire's letter tell us about the way that black boys were regarded and treated by families like hers in the eighteenth century? Consider for instance:
      (i)   the terms she uses to describe her black boy
      (ii)   her reasons for wanting to get rid of him
      (iii)   the arguments she uses to persuade her mother to have him.

4   It was quite common for a lady to have her 'little black boy' educated (at least taught to read and write) and baptised.
    a   How can we tell that Pompey had been (i) educated and (ii) baptised?
    b   Why do you think that his mistress had these things done?

5   a   Do you think that the letter published in *The Tatler* and signed 'Pompey' was really written by a six-year-old boy? Consider, for example, the style in which it is written. If you do not think that it was, who do you think did write it, and why?
    b   Whether or not the letter was really written by a six-year-old boy called Pompey, does it give us an accurate picture of the way in which young black servant boys were regarded and treated at this time?

Test the evidence by doing the following exercise. Divide your page into three columns. Head these as set out below. The first column has been completed for you. Complete the other two.

Black servant boys	What Pompey had to say	Other evidence in the chapter
Age		
Religion		
Dress		
Collar		
How they were regarded by their mistresses		

Above   James Drummond, 2nd Duke of Perth
Right   Charles, 3rd Duke of Richmond, with Lennox, his servant.
Both these pictures show black boys with white masters, but they appear to show two very different kinds of relationships.
Study the pictures carefully, and note down the points which seem to suggest a difference in the way that each boy was regarded by his master

Imaginative exercise
Write on *one* of the following:
Imagine you are an ordinary footboy in the same household as Pompey (whose duties are those as described by Charles Dickens). Do you envy Pompey his position, or do you feel sorry for him? Explain in detail why you feel as you do.

Imagine you are the black boy who was employed by the Duchess of Kingston. You are now on your way to the West Indies. What are your thoughts and feelings about how life – and the Duchess of Kingston – have treated you?

6 TINKER, TAILOR, SOLDIER, SAILOR...

... the first fine Spanish needles in England were made in the reign of Queen Mary (1688–94), in Cheapside, by a negro; but such his envy, that he would teach his art to none; so that it died with him.

Thomas Fuller, *Worthies of England*, 1840

This is just one of the many scattered pieces of evidence which show that, although the majority of black people who lived in Britain during the seventeenth and eighteenth centuries worked as domestic servants, many were also to be found in a great variety of other occupations. Chance references in newspapers provide us with some other clues. The *St James's Evening Post* of 21–24 May 1726, for example, mentions 'a Negro who was Harrowing with 3 horses in a Field', and *The London Chronicle* of 6 January 1787 mentions 'a Black Hairdresser' who also appears to have kept a lodging house.

Two other black men we know of who set up in business were the famous Ignatius Sancho (whom we met in chapter 3) and Cesar Picton, who had also been an upper servant in a wealthy family for many years.

Ignatius Sancho and his wife set up in a 'shop of grocery' at 20 Charles Street, Westminster in 1773. Although he was already suffering from gout, overweight and general ill-health, he wrote to a friend:

... I verily think the happiest part of my life is to come – soap, starch, and blue, with raisins, figs, etc. – we shall cut a respectable figure. . . .

Letter to Mrs H. 1 November 1773
Letter XVI, *Letters of the late Ignatius Sancho*

He does not seem to have done very well commercially, however, as frequent complaints in his letters to friends show us. In 1777, for instance, he described himself as 'a poor starving black Negro, with six children' and in November 1779 he wrote that he was:

... never poorer since created — But 'tis a general case — Blessed times for a poor Blacky grocer to hang or drown in!

Letter CXIV, *Letters of the late Ignatius Sancho*

Through his wide interests and knowledge of art, music, literature and the theatre, Ignatius was very well-known, and his shop became the meeting place for some of the most famous writers, artists, actors and even politicians of the day. This did not protect him and his family, though, from racial abuse from other people. In another of his letters he tells how, coming home one day, 'they stopped us in the town, and most generously insulted us' until, encouraged by his wife, he 'ventured his head out of the coach door, and swore liberally'.

Cesar Picton, though he did not find fame, made quite a fortune for himself. With a £100 legacy from his former employer, and almost certainly some savings, he set up as a coal merchant in Kingston-upon-Thames in 1788. He did so well that when he died in 1836 he left a considerable amount of property, including one house with shops and a wharf attached, and another with a garden, stables, coach house and two acres of land.

Cesar Picton's signature as witness to a deed in January 1816

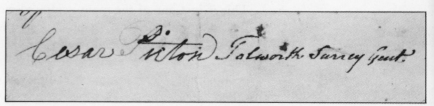

At the other end of the business scale, some black boys managed to become apprentices in order to learn a trade. In 1731, however, the City of London tried to put a stop to this, by issuing the following proclamation:

> *It is Ordered by this Court, That for the future no Negroes or other Blacks be ... bound Apprentices at any of the Companies of this City (or) to any Freeman thereof; and that Copies of this Order be printed and sent to the Masters and Wardens of the several Companies of this City....*
> Proclamation by the Lord Mayor of London, 14 September 1731

From the end of the seventeenth century at least there were black soldiers in the British army, many of whom were regimental bandsmen.

There were also black sailors in the British navy (like Frank Barber), and many who were seamen on British merchant ships, especially those engaged in trade with Africa.

Over the years, many of these – mainly African – merchant sailors 'jumped ship' in Britain, and so became members of the black community which grew up, particularly in areas such as the eastern riverside parishes of London, during the eighteenth century. Many, however, only stayed until their return journeys, putting up at the lodging houses in the dockland areas of London and other seaports such as Bristol and Liverpool. One man who showed himself to be the friend of such people was a Stepney clergyman, Dr Mayo. After his death in 1791, one of his curates wrote of him:

> *He was particularly kind to the negroes, and uninstructed men of colour who, employed generally on board of ships, occasionally*

An eighteenth century regimental band.
How many black men can you see in the band and what instruments are they playing?

One of the many black sailors on British ships. What appears to be his job?

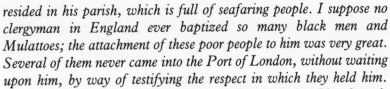

resided in his parish, which is full of seafaring people. I suppose no clergyman in England ever baptized so many black men and Mulattoes; the attachment of these poor people to him was very great. Several of them never came into the Port of London, without waiting upon him, by way of testifying the respect in which they held him.

Obituary Notice of Dr Mayo in *The Orthodox Churchman's Magazine*, 1802

Throughout the period of slavery, many people, both black and white, believed that a Christian could not be a slave – although the law on the matter was never clear. As a result, while many white people had their slaves baptised as Christians, others forbade it. And many black people, believing that it would help them either to become or to remain free, applied to clergymen to baptise them.

Questions

1 a What do you think Ignatius Sancho meant when he wrote: 'we shall cut a respectable figure'?
   b Did he and his wife succeed? Quote evidence to support your answer.
2 What two types of evidence show that Cesar Picton did manage to 'cut a respectable figure'?
3 a Describe two instances of racial prejudice for which evidence is presented in this chapter.
   b Which would you say is the more serious instance? Why?

For discussion

Suggest reasons why black men during the period became each of the following: army bandsmen; sailors on British ships; boxers.

Tom Molineaux fighting Tom Crib in 1811. Tom Molineaux, who arrived in London from Virginia, penniless, in 1809, was just one of several black boxers in nineteenth century Britain

Lastly, let us look at: *A Narrative of the Most Remarkable Particulars in the Life of James Albert Ukawsaw Gronniosaw, an African Prince, as Related by Himself*. This book, which was published in Bath, in England, around 1770, tells the story of one black man who, on coming to England a free man, found that he had exchanged the injustice and hardships of slavery in America for those facing many thousands of poor people (both black and white) in Britain around the middle of the eighteenth century.*

Ukawsaw had decided to come to England as he 'imagined that all the Inhabitants of this Island were Holy'. (Perhaps missionaries had given him this idea.) When he arrived at Portsmouth, therefore, he

* As such, it is of great interest and value, as we have very little first-hand evidence regarding the lives of poor people in general in the eighteenth century, and even less regarding poor black people.

received a most considerable shock. First of all, he was astonished to hear the natives of England swearing and cursing. And then, even worse, he found himself among people 'who defrauded me of my money and watch; [so that] all my promis'd happiness was blasted'.

When he moved to London, therefore, and lodged at a house in Petticoat Lane, he was much more cautious about trusting people. So much so that when he met there a woman called Betty, who was a weaver, he was at first afraid that she would be:

> *like all the rest I had met with at Portsmouth etc. and which had almost given me a dislike to all white women. But after a short acquaintance I had the happiness to find that she was very different, and quite sincere.*

> Ukawsaw Gronniosaw

So he married her. However, soon after their marriage, their 'many great troubles and difficulties' began. Ukawsaw says that 'I ... was never so happy as when I had something to do', but unfortunately he found himself for long spells unemployed, and therefore without any money. His wife had been earning good money as a weaver, but soon after their marriage he made her give up her job because riots broke out amongst the workers, and he was afraid that:

> *they should insist on my joining the rioters which I could not think of, and, possibly, if I had refused to do so they would have knocked me on the head.*

So they moved to Colchester, where he became a road-worker. But when winter came, the job came to an end, so that both he and his wife were unemployed again. By this time they had a young baby:

> *The winter prov'd remarkably severe, and we were reduc'd to the greatest distress imaginable.*

Ukawsaw tried to get work as a farm labourer, but without success. For several days they had nothing to eat but four very large carrots, which someone had given them. Then, 'by almost a miracle' they were rescued by a man called Peter Daniel, whom Ukawsaw had met while he was working on the roads. Hearing that Ukawsaw had lost his job, Peter Daniel feared that he would be in want, and sent for him. Daniel gave him a guinea and, better still, employed him to pull down a house and rebuild it.

Ukawsaw was then offered work with better wages in Norwich, so they moved there. His wife hired a loom, and by both working very hard they began 'to do very well' – until fresh misfortune struck. Their three children became ill with smallpox, and one of them died. Ukawsaw had great difficulty in finding a church minister who would bury his daughter. One said he could not because the family were not members of his church, another that the child had not been baptised. As a result, by the time she was buried, and the other two children had recovered, he was several weeks behind with the rent. His landlady threatened that 'she would turn us all into the street' if he did not settle up straight away.

This time Ukawsaw was helped by a man called Henry Gurdney, who was a Quaker. Hearing of the family's distress, he paid all their overdue rent, and helped Ukawsaw back into employment by advising him:

To follow the employ of chopping chaff, and bought me an instrument for that purpose. There were but few people in the town that made this their business beside myself; so that I did very well indeed and we became easy and happy. But we did not continue long in this comfortable state: Many of the inferior people were envious and ill-natur'd and set up the employ and worked under price on purpose to get my business from me, and they succeeded so well that I could hardly get anything to do, and became again unfortunate.

So Ukawsaw moved again, this time to Kidderminster, where a man named Watson employed him 'in twisting silk and worsted together'. Betty had not joined him immediately, and had been taken ill, so that when she did leave Norwich she had to sell all they possessed to pay the bills which had mounted during her illness.

It is at this point that Ukawsaw ends his *Narrative:*

Such is our situation at present. My wife, by hard labour at the loom, does everything that can be expected from her towards the maintenance of our family; and God is pleased to incline the hearts of his People at times to yield us their charitable assistances; being myself through age and infirmity able to contribute but little to their support. As Pilgrims, and very poor Pilgrims, we are travelling through many difficulties.

Questions

4   Explain how Ukawsaw Gronniosaw and his wife tried to overcome their poverty, and suggest reasons why they found this so difficult.

5   a   Why, do you think, do we have 'very little first-hand evidence regarding the lives of poor people in general in the eighteenth century'?

     b   Why do we have even less evidence about the lives of poor black people?

     c   Suggest reasons why Ukawsaw Gronniosaw (i) was able to write his autobiography at a time when most poor people could neither read nor write and (ii) wanted to write his autobiography.

7 SOLDIER, SAILOR, BEGGARMAN...

Tom and Jerry 'Masquerading it' among the Cadgers in the 'Back Slums' in the Holy Land *by George Cruickshank. This cartoon shows the kind of pub or club where the London poor used to meet to cook, eat, drink, keep warm and make merry. Often called 'thieves kitchens', they were in fact used by all sorts of people. The black man seated on the right was nick-named Massa Piebald because of his black face and white hair; left of centre is Black Billy Waters who was at that time 'King of the Beggars'*

As the eighteenth century wore on, more and more black people joined the ranks of the poor white people who lived packed together in the back streets and slums of East London. Among them were many seamen, as we saw in the last chapter. Many others were 'runaway slaves', i.e. those who had chosen freedom and poverty rather than remain slaves. Others were former slaves or servants of white people who had abandoned them or thrown them out. Such people managed to make or scrape a living in a variety of ways, though few, it seems, turned to crime (other than begging, which was against the law).

Some became crossing-sweepers – people who swept a path across the then filthy streets for anyone who could afford to pay them.

Others became beggars or street musicians. It was even said that black beggars had all the best pitches, and that they were so successful that white beggars sometimes blackened themselves in order to improve their takings.

One very successful black beggar was Charles M'Gee, who was born in Jamaica in 1744. He had lost one eye and his hair was almost white:

This singular man usually stands at the Obelisk, at the foot of Ludgate-Hill. . . . His stand is certainly above all others the most popular, many thousands of persons crossing it in the course of the day.

John Thomas Smith, *Vagabondiana, or Mendicant Wanderers through the Streets of London . . .*, 1817

Black and white crossing sweepers taking a break!

The Ethiopian Serenaders.
One of the bands of white street musicians who disguised themselves as black men in the middle of the nineteenth century. Why do you think that they did this?

The funeral of 'Black Billy Waters, King of the Beggars' from the broadsheet The Death, Funeral and Last Will of Black Billy.
How does the picture tell us that Billy Waters was popular among the people of London?
Why, do you think, was he so popular among London's beggars?

When he died in the early nineteenth century, he left several hundred pounds to a Miss Waithman, who, on passing him, had not only always given him a penny or a halfpenny, but had given it with a smile.

Another who was very successful was Billy Waters, a street violinist or 'gut-scraper', as he liked to be called. His pitch was outside the Adelphi Theatre in the Strand, where he collected a great quantity of 'browne' (halfpennies). Said to be known by every child in London, he was so popular that he was elected 'King' by other London beggars, a short time before his death in 1823.

Not all black people who lived among London's poor were as lucky as Billy Waters. Most lived a miserable existence. There is evidence, though, that black people in Britain's cities did much to support one another in times of trouble. When for instance, two black men were sent to prison in London for begging in 1773, it was reported by the *General Evening Post* that they were 'visited by upwards of 300 of their countrymen' and that the black community 'contributed largely towards their support during their confinement'.

Exercise
Imagine that you are a runaway slave in London. Explain: why you have run away from your master or mistress; why you intend to stay free; why you expect life among London's poor to be hard; who you expect to help you, and why.

After 1783, the number of poor black people in London was greatly increased by the arrival of black American Loyalists. These were men who had fought on the side of the British in the American War of Independence, in return for the promise of freedom from slavery. When the British lost, these black soldiers found, like many white Loyalists, that they had to take refuge outside the newly independent United States of America. Once in London, however, most found that they had freedom – but nothing else.

The Government had set up schemes to grant pensions or sums of money to American Loyalists who had taken refuge in Britain, but the commissioners running them were reluctant to help the black Loyalists, feeling that as they had 'gained their Liberty' in the war, they had 'no right to ask or expect anything from the Government'.

Peter Anderson was a black American Loyalist. When he at first applied to the pension commissioners for help, he was denied it. So he got a white man, Lord Dunmore, to support his claim, and was then granted £10. This did not last long, however, so in a few months he was applying to the commissioners again. He told them that:

> *I endeavour'd to get work but cannot get Any I am Thirty Nine Years of Age and am ready and Willing to serve His Britinack Majesty While I am Able But I am really starvin about the Streets Having Nobody to give me a Morsal of bread and dare not go home to my Own Country again.*

The plight of destitute people like Peter Anderson was made even worse by the very severe winter which occurred in 1785–86, so much so that early in 1786 an appeal was made to the public to subscribe to an emergency fund for their relief. The appeal was launched by a committee which became known as the Committee for the Relief of the Black Poor, and which was made up of merchants, bankers and Members of Parliament. The public response was so generous that by 18 April enough money had been collected to help '460 Persons'. On 15 March the Committee reported that:

> *From the 24th January, when they began to give broth, a piece of meat, and a two-penny loaf to each person, they have relieved 140 every day, (and from) the 5th February . . . 210 daily, besides bread sent everyday, to many who were sick at home. They have between 40*

and 50 in . . . Hospital. . . . About 250 have had shoes and stockings:
to many have been given shoes, trowsers and jackets. Some have been
fitted out, and sent to sea, and a place is provided with straw and
blankets for such as apply for Lodging.

The Morning Post, 15 March 1786

It was not long, however, before it seemed to the Committee that it
would be better for Britain if the 'Black Poor' were removed rather
than continue to receive relief. At a meeting on 10 May 1786,
therefore, the Committee decided to take up the suggestion of a man
named Henry Smeathman to found a colony in Sierra Leone on the
West Coast of Africa for the re-settlement of Britain's black population. Despite government support, this scheme failed. Ottobah
Cugoano, a leader of Britain's black community at the time, had the
following to say about the scheme and about the reasons for its failure:

This prospect of settling a free colony to Great-Britain in a peaceable
alliance with the inhabitants at Sierra Leone, has . . . (not) alto-
gether met with the . . . (approval) of the Africans here. . . . Had a
treaty of agreement been first made with the inhabitants of Africa,
and the terms and nature of such a settlement fixed upon, and its
situation and boundary pointed out; then might the Africans, and
others here, have embarked with a good prospect of enjoying
happiness and prosperity. . . .
. . . Many more of the Black People still in this country would have,
with great gladness, embraced the opportunity, longing to reach their
native land; but as the old saying is, A burnt child dreads the fire. . . .
For can it be readily . . . (believed) that (the) government would
establish a free colony for them nearly on the spot . . . (where) it
supports . . . forts and garrisons, to ensnare, merchandize, and to
carry others into captivity and slavery.

Ottobah Cugoano, *Thoughts and Sentiments on the Evil of*
Slavery, 1787

Exercise
Imagine that you are a reporter on an eighteenth century
newspaper. Choose *two* of the following headlines and write
reports for your newspaper about the stories to which they refer. In
each case explain the background to the story, and then the
arguments on both sides of the issue.
   Black American Loyalist Refused Help
   Cold Winter – Warm Hearts: Public Response to Emergency
   Appeal
   Re-settlement of Britain's Black Poor – is it the right answer?

---

8 THE CASE AGAINST SLAVERY IN BRITAIN

As we saw in chapter 1, it was never clear, until slavery was abolished throughout the British Empire by an Act of Parliament of 1833, whether or not it was legal to hold people as slaves in Britain. Lawyers argued and disagreed. Judges, trying various cases which came before them, made different judgements on the matter. Here are some of the legal opinions stated over the years:

1569   *... it was resolved, that England was too pure an air for Slaves to breathe in.*

1701   *... as soon as a Negro comes to England, he becomes free; one may be a villein in England but not a slave.*

1701   *... the Laws of England take not notice of a Negroe.*

1706   *... By the common law no man can have property in another.*

1729   *... a slave coming from the West-Indies to Great Britain, doth not become free ... also ... his Master may legally compel him to return again to the Plantations.*

villein: tenant bound to the Lord of his manor

(The 'Laws of England' meant the laws of Wales also. Scotland, though part of Great Britain, had separate laws.)

One man who tried to end the uncertainty, and have slavery in England and Wales made clearly illegal, was Granville Sharp. The whole matter was brought to his attention by a chance meeting one day with Jonathan Strong.

Jonathan Strong, a black boy aged about seventeen, had been brought from Barbados to London by a lawyer and planter named David Lisle. In 1765, for what reason we do not know, Lisle had beaten Jonathan about the head with a pistol, so savagely that he became ill with fever and nearly blind. In this condition Lisle threw him out on to the street, where he had to ask help from a stranger:

I met with a man – told him my case: he recommended (me) to Mr. William Sharp in Mincing Lane ... I took his advice, and went to Mr. Sharp, I could hardly walk, or see my way, where I was going. When I came to him, and he saw me in that condition, the gentleman take charity of me, and gave me some stuff to wash my eyes with, and some money to get myself a little necessaries till the next day. The day after, I come to the gentleman, and he sent me into hospital; and I was there four months and a half. All the while I was in the hospital, the gentleman find me ... clothes, shoes, and stockings, and when I come out, He paid for my lodging, and ... money to find myself some necessaries; till he get me into a place.

Testimony given in Court by Jonathan Strong

Granville Sharp

Granville Sharp was William Sharp's brother, and just happened to be leaving his brother's surgery that day when Jonathan was queuing up with other poor people for the free medical treatment which they knew William Sharp would give them.

The place which the Sharp brothers found Jonathan when he left St Bartholomew's hospital was as an errand boy for Mr Brown, a 'surgeon and apothecary' in Fenchurch Street. Mr Brown paid him wages, and Jonathan 'grew to be a stout good-looking young man'. Two years later, however, when he was completely recovered, he was spotted by his former master, Lisle. Seeing that his 'property' was now restored in value, Lisle found out where Jonathan lived. He then employed two slave-hunters to kidnap him and have him put into prison. There he was to stay until a ship was ready to sail to the West Indies – for Lisle had already sold him, in his absence, to a Jamaican planter for £30.

Jonathan was now in a situation familiar to many black people in eighteenth century Britain. For whether, like Jonathan, they had been abandoned, whether they had run away, or whether they had always been free, they were in constant danger of capture or recapture by slave-hunters. And he now took the course of action taken by all kidnapped black people who had been baptised (see chapter 6) – he sent for his godparents to help him.

Jonathan's godfathers came – but were refused admission to him. He therefore sent in desperation to Granville Sharp, as he had shown such an interest in him before. Granville Sharp was also denied admission, but did not give up, and finally managed to see him. When he heard Jonathan's story he was so shocked that he applied to the Court for his release.

The result was that on 18 September 1767 the Lord Mayor and Chief Magistrate of the City of London discharged Jonathan from custody.

David Lisle, however, would not let the matter drop. He charged the Sharp brothers with robbery, and challenged Granville Sharp to a duel. Sharp refused the latter challenge, but told him: 'You are a lawyer, and you shall want no satisfaction which law can give you'.

In charging the Sharp brothers with robbery, Lisle was insisting that Jonathan Strong had been his *property*. The brothers' defence was that it was unlawful to hold people as property, i.e. as slaves, in England and Wales. When they consulted lawyers, however, they found that the law was unclear. Nevertheless, Granville Sharp 'could not believe that the Laws of England were really so injurious to natural Rights' and so set about a study of them – though he had 'never opened a lawbook (except the Bible)', he said, in his life. His study took him nearly two years, but in the end satisfied him that he had been right in the first place: slavery was not allowed by English law. 'God be thanked', he said. He wrote his findings down in a book. (See illustration of title page on page 38.)

The title page of Granville Sharp's book.
What inspired Granville Sharp in his fight against slavery?

This was enough to frighten Lisle into dropping his case. But for Granville Sharp the fight had just begun – for it was to be nothing less than a fight against slavery in England and Wales.

Over the next few years, Granville Sharp used his influence and the law to rescue several black men who had been kidnapped in England to be sold abroad as slaves. It was not until 1772, however, that a case came to court which Sharp hoped would settle the issue as to whether it was lawful to hold people as slaves in England and Wales. This was the case of James Somerset, who had been brought to England from the USA in 1769. Later, he had claimed his freedom by running away from his master, who had then had him kidnapped and taken on board a ship to be sold as a slave in Jamaica.

Since the laws in Scotland were, and are, separate from those in England and Wales, a separate case was needed to decide the matter in Scotland. This occurred in 1778, in the case of Knight versus Wedderburn. Knight, a black man, had been brought from Jamaica to Scotland when he was about twelve. He later married and seemed contented in his position as Wedderburn's personal servant, but after some years he left him, declaring that he was a free man. Wedderburn claimed that Knight was, however, 'his servant for life' and had him arrested. The matter came before the Sheriff of Perthshire, who decided that personal service for life just meant slavery, and that slavery was not allowed by law in Scotland. This decision was later confirmed by the Court of Session, the highest court of justice in Scotland. Slavery was therefore declared illegal in Scotland.

Some of Somerset's friends managed to release him from the ship, and his case came before Chief Justice Lord Mansfield in January 1772, Granville Sharp having arranged his defence.

Lord Mansfield had previously, in trying several similar cases, found in favour of the slave owners, thus delivering the black people involved up to slavery in the West Indies. In summing up a case in that same year, in fact, he had even said that he did not want the law on the matter made clear:

I don't know what the consequences may be, if the masters were to lose their property by . . . bringing their slaves to England. I hope it will never be finally discussed, for I would have all masters think them free and all Negroes think they were not, because they would both behave better.

On 22 June 1772, however, Lord Mansfield finally delivered his judgement, which was that:

No master was ever allowed here to take a slave by force to be sold abroad *because he deserted from his service, or for any other reason whatever* ... *and therefore the man must be discharged.*

This judgement clearly did not go so far as to declare slavery to be unlawful, though Granville Sharp and other opponents of slavery had hoped that it would – and many people, both at the time and since, thought that it did. Moreover, though it made it illegal for them to do so, it did not even put a stop to slave-owners forcibly shipping black men and women to slavery abroad – as newspaper and other reports show us. *Bonner's Bristol Journal* of 8 December 1792, for instance, reported the case of a black servant girl who had been sold for £80 Jamaican currency, after many years in her master's service:

A bystander who saw her put on board the boat at Lamplighter's Hall says, 'her tears flowed down her face like a shower of rain'.

Lord Mansfield's judgement did, however, spare one black man, James Somerset, from West Indian slavery; and London's black community, which had followed the case closely, and made sure that there was always a black delegation in court, celebrated the victory. According to a report in *The London Packet*, about two hundred black people gathered a few days afterwards:

... at a public house in Westminster, to celebrate the triumph which their brother Somerset had obtained over Mr. Stewart his master. Lord Mansfield's health was echoed round the room, and the evening was concluded with a ball. The tickets to this Black assembly were 5s. each.

Questions

1 What do you think was meant by: 'England was too pure an air for slaves to breathe in'?
2 Read Lord Mansfield's summing up of a case in 1772. Explain in your own words why he did not want the case on slavery made clear. What do you think of his reason?
3 Why did many people believe that Lord Mansfield's judgement had made slavery illegal in England and Wales?

---

9 BLACK PEOPLE AGAINST SLAVERY

We have seen how, throughout the period when there was slavery in Britain, many black people resisted or rebelled against being regarded as property – if necessary by running away from their 'owners'. We have also seen how those who made up the poor but free black communities of London and elsewhere showed a great deal of support for one another, especially in times of trouble. This support no doubt included giving shelter and assistance to any who had just claimed their freedom. In these ways black people showed, through their actions, their opposition to slavery and to other unjust treatment. There were also many who raised their voices, and some who used the power of writing to protest against the enslavement of black people – either in Britain or anywhere else in the world.

Ignatius Sancho mentioned slavery in several of the many letters which he wrote to friends. In 1778, for instance, he commented that: 'The grand object of English navigators – indeed of all Christian navigators – is money-money-money-' and that the lives of the natives of Africa were made miserable by:

> *... the Christians' abominable Traffic for slaves – and the horrid cruelty and treachery of the petty Kings – encouraged by their Christian customers – who carry them strong liquors, to enflame their national madness – and powder and bad fire-arms, to furnish them with the hellish means of killing and kidnapping.*
> Letter LXVIII, *Letters of the late Ignatius Sancho*, 1782

Phillis Wheatley, an African girl who had been kidnapped and taken to New England, USA, at the age of eight, became well-known both there and in England as a poet. Aged about nineteen, she visited England in 1772 as the guest of various members of the English aristocracy, and her book of *Poems on various subjects* was published in London in 1773. On 16 May 1789, the London daily newspaper *The Diary* published one of her poems. In it she explained that her 'love of FREEDOM sprung' from a personal knowledge of slavery:

> *I, young in life, by seeming cruel fate,*
> *Was snatch'd from AFRIC's fancy'd happy seat;*
> *What pangs excruciating must molest,*
> *What sorrows labour in my parents' breast?*
> *Steel'd was that soul and by no mis'ry mov'd*
> *That from a father seiz'd his babe belove'd;*
> *Such-such my case; and can I then but pray*
> *Others may never feel tyrannic sway?*

Phillis Wheatley

Ottobah Cugoano was born in 1757 in the part of Africa now called Ghana. In 1770 he was kidnapped and taken to the West Indies, where he spent ten months in 'dreadful captivity and horrible slavery' in Grenada. He was brought to England in 1772, and soon became one of the leaders of London's black community. In 1787 he published a short book in which he set out the case for the Abolition of the slave trade. Called *Thoughts and Sentiments on the Evil and Wicked Traffic of the Human Species*, he included in it his memories of slavery in Grenada:

(Every day I saw) the most dreadful scenes of misery and cruelty . . . my miserable companions often cruelly lashed, and as it were cut to pieces, for the most trifling faults . . . I saw a slave receive twenty-four lashes of the whip for being seen in church on a Sunday instead of going to work.

He wrote that Britain should be the first to abolish the slave trade and to free the slaves under her control, and explained why:

Britain having now acquired a greater share in that iniquitous commerce than all the rest together, they are the first that ought to set an example.

Cugoano, with other members of Britain's black community, also wrote many letters to English people who could help, or who had helped, the cause of Abolition. In April 1789 nine men wrote to Mr William Dickson, who had been Private Secretary to the Governor of Barbados, and who had just written a book called *Letters on Slavery*. This book, the writers of the letter said, gave:

but too just a picture of the Slave Trade, and the horrid cruelties practised on the . . . people in the West Indies, to the disgrace of Christianity. . .
It is the duty of every man who is a friend to religion and humanity . . . to shew his detestation of such inhuman traffick. . .
Permit us, Sir, on behalf of ourselves and the rest of our brethren, to offer you our sincere thanks for the testimony of regard you have shewn . . . We are,
Sir, . . .
Olaudah Equiano, or Gustavus Vassa
Ottobah Cugoano, or John Suarr
Yahne Aelane, or Joseph Sanders
Broughwar Jogensmel, or Jasper Goree
Cojoh Ammere, or George Williams
Thomas Cooper
William Greek
George Mandeville
Bernard Elliot Griffiths

Olaudah Equiano c. 1789

Olaudah Equiano, whose signature appears first on this letter, was the best known black Abolitionist in eighteenth-century Britain. He had been born in 1745 'in a charming fruitful vale name Essaka' in the part of Africa which is now called Nigeria. Slave-hunters kidnapped him when he was eleven, took him on a long journey to the coast, and put him on board a slave ship where he first caught sight of 'white men with horrible looks, red faces, and loose hair'. Although he spent the next ten years as a slave, and was bought and sold several times, he was fortunate in that he did not have to endure for long the horrors of life on a plantation. He was bought by a naval captain and so spent much of his time at sea, both on warships and on trading vessels. Besides seamanship he learnt how to read and write, to do arithmetic, to 'shave and dress hair' and to trade for himself. During some time spent in England he was baptised and went to school.

In 1766 he was able to buy his freedom from his 'owner' with his own savings, and during the following eleven years or so he led a life of the most extraordinary variety and adventure. Again spending most of his time at sea, he visited Italy, Spain, Portugal, Turkey, the West Indies, the USA and the Arctic. He witnessed the eruption of the volcano Vesuvius, was offered (and refused) two wives in Turkey, narrowly escaped re-enslavement and death in the USA, and was shipwrecked in the Bahamas. During his time at sea he worked as an able seaman, as a steward, and also, once, as acting captain. A very religious man, Equiano once even tried (though unsuccessfully) to become a missionary.

We know all this because Olaudah Equiano, like Ukawsaw Gronniosaw, wrote his autobiography. First published in London in 1789, it has now been published in over twenty editions, including translations into Dutch and German.

On its publication Equiano travelled all over the British Isles, both to promote sales of his book and to further the cause of the abolition of slavery and the slave trade. Indeed, the former did much to help the latter, as this entry in *A Century of Birmingham Life* points out:

Gustavus Vassa (Olaudah Equiano), the African, visited Birmingham this year (1789), and increased the indignation of the friends of the slaves by the circulation of his narrative.

The following extract from one of his letters shows us just how active Equiano was in the fight for Abolition, and also suggests how valuable his work for that fight was:

London Feby the 27.th 1792
Dr. Revd. & Worthy friends etc.
*   This with my Best of Respects to you and wife . . . and also your Little Lovely Daughter – I thank you for all kindnesses which you was please to show me, may God ever Reward you for it – Sir, I went to Ireland and was there 8½ months and sold 1900 copies of my*

*narrtive. I came here on the 10th ... and I now mean ... to leave
London in about 8 or 10 Days ... and take me a Wife (one Miss
Cullen) of Soham in Cambridgeshire – and when I have given her
about 8 or 10 Days Comfort, I mean Directly to go to Scotland – and
sell my 5th. Editions – I Trust that my going about has been of much
use to the Cause of the Abolition of the accursed Slave Trade – a
Gentleman of the Committee the Revd. Dr. Baker has said that I am
more use to the Cause than half the People in the Country – I wish to
God, I could be so.... – May the Lord Bless all the friends of
Humanity. – I will be Glad to see you at my Wedg [wedding].*

  I am with all Due Respects
    ... Gustavus Vassa The African
P.S.... Pray mind the Africans from the Pulpits.

It was to be another fifteen years (1807) before Parliament made it
illegal for any British person to take part in the slave trade, and it was
not until 1833 that *slavery* was made illegal throughout the British
Empire – for those who made most profit from the slave trade and
from slave labour on the plantations had more power of persuasion
than the 'friends of Humanity' to whom Equiano referred, i.e.
members and supporters of the Society for the Abolition of the Slave
Trade.

Meanwhile, however, Equiano and other black Abolitionists lent
their support to a Bill brought before Parliament in 1788 (and which
was eventually passed) to regulate the conditions under which
Africans were transported to slavery in the West Indies. They
followed the debates in both Houses of Parliament, and Equiano was
consulted by several Members of Parliament during the time that the
Bill was going through.

In addition to this work, Equiano wrote very many letters on the
subject of Abolition to the press, to politicians – and even to the
Queen.

In 1786 Equiano was recommended to the Commissioners of his
Majesty's Navy as a 'proper person' to superintend part of the Sierra
Leone Scheme (see chapter 7), and accompany to Africa those black
people who had been persuaded to leave Britain to live in the new
colony. He was not keen to go, as he explained in his autobiography:

*I pointed out to them many objections to my going ... particularly
I expressed some difficulties on account of the slave dealers, as I
would certainly oppose their traffic in the human species by every
means in my power.*

His objections, however, 'were overruled' and he was appointed as
'Commissary for Stores for the Black Poor going to Sierra Leone' in
November 1786.

On taking up his duties he discovered that the agent was taking
money for stores which he was not supplying:

I could not silently suffer government to be thus cheated, and my countrymen plundered and oppressed, and even left destitute ... I therefore informed the Commissioners of the Navy of the agent's proceedings; but my dismission [dismissal] was soon after procured, by means of a gentlemen ∴ whom the agent ... had deceived...

Thus ended my part of the long-talked-of expedition to Sierra Leone....

Equiano had worked closely at times with Granville Sharp, not only in the campaign for the abolition of the slave trade, but also in individual cases of black people kidnapped in Britain. And it is from Sharp, that pioneer white Abolitionist, that we have the last evidence regarding Equiano, Britain's foremost black Abolitionist. It is not known exactly when he died, but some years later, in 1811, Sharp wrote in a letter to his niece:

He was a sober, honest man – and I went to see him when he lay upon his death bed, and had lost his voice so that he could only whisper...

Questions

1   Ignatius Sancho and Olaudah Equiano both referred in their writing to the slave trade.
    a   Ignatius Sancho blamed two groups of people for the trade. (i) Who were they? (ii) Which group, did he say, encouraged the other, and how?
    b   In objecting to being appointed to superintend the Sierra Leone scheme, Olaudah Equiano mentioned 'the slave dealers'. (i) Who do you think he meant? (ii) What, would you say, was his attitude towards them?
2   Both Olaudah Equiano and Ukawsaw Gronniosaw (see chapter 6) wrote autobiographies which were published in the eighteenth century. Today that of Olaudah Equiano is much better known than that of Ukawsaw Gronniosaw. Suggest reasons why this is so.
3   a   How, do you think, did Olaudah Equiano's travels round the country help the sales of his autobiography?
    b   In what ways, do you think, did sales of the book further the cause of the abolition of slavery and the slave trade?
4   Which of the pieces of writing by black people quoted in this chapter do you think may have helped most in the flight against slavery and the slave trade? Give reasons for your answer.

BLACK ANCESTORS IN BRITAIN

At the end of the eighteenth century there were still about 10,000 black people in Britain. What became of them? They married and were absorbed into the white population. Their children are now white, with no inkling of their African blood and ancestry.
> Folarin Shyllon, *Black People in Britain 1555–1833*, 1977

Most of this book has been concerned with answering the question: what was life like for the black people who lived in Britain in the seventeenth, eighteenth and nineteenth centuries? As you have seen, answers to this question can be found in documentary and pictorial evidence. The quotation above gives one modern historian's answers to two other questions which face anyone trying to uncover the history of black people in Britain. First, what was the size of the black population? Second, why did it decline in the nineteenth century? Let us look more closely at how these questions can be answered.

The size of the black population

We have no accurate knowledge of the numbers of black people in Britain at any time during the period covered by this book. Even contemporary observers could only make guesses, for there were no official figures to help them. (The first census, or official count, of the population of England and Wales was carried out in 1801). In the 1760s and 1770s estimates were made which differed widely, and which appear to have been based largely on the numbers of black people seen by the observers. They ranged from 14 000 to 30 000 (in 1765) for the whole kingdom, and from 14 000 to 20 000 (in 1764) for London alone. In *Black People in Britain 1555–1833* Folarin Shyllon has summed up the matter like this:

In 1768 Granville Sharp, who, more than any other Englishman in Britain at the time, was perhaps qualified to give the most reliable estimate, accepted 20,000 as the population of blacks in Britain. But the figure of 20,000 seems rather too high. The black population during the eighteenth century was in a constant state of flux. While some blacks were arriving from the West Indies and America, others were returning. Ill-treatment, starvation, disease, and poverty took their toll among those who formed the 'permanent' black population. After weighing all these factors carefully, it seems that the black population in Britain throughout the eighteenth century at any given time could not have exceeded 10,000.

a In 1801 the population of England and Wales was just under nine millions. The population of Scotland was about one and a half millions.

Taking 10 000 to be the number of black people in Britain, construct a *bar chart* to show the proportion of black people in the population of Britain at the beginning of the 19th century.

b The population of London in 1801 was 900 000. Taking 9 000 to be the number of black people living in London, construct a *bar chart* to show the proportion of black people in London at the beginning of the nineteenth century.

c What do the two charts tell you about the *distribution* of black people in Britain at the beginning of the nineteenth century?

For discussion

Why did estimates for the number of black people in Britain in the eighteenth century differ so widely?

What reasons do you think people had for making these estimates?

How might these reasons have affected the accuracy of the estimates?

How could estimates made today be any more accurate?

The decline of the black population after 1800

In chapter 2 we looked at the question of why black people had come to Britain in the first place, and why their numbers had grown during the seventeenth and eighteenth centuries. We found that the answers lay in Britain's part in the slave trade, and in the great prosperity of the West Indian sugar colonies. It is therefore not surprising that the falling fortunes of the West Indian sugar planters in the early nineteenth century, and the abolition of the British slave trade and, later, of slavery in the British Empire, reduced the numbers of black people coming to Britain. After the abolition of the slave trade by an Act of Parliament of 1807, those slaves already in the West Indies became too valuable to be brought to Britain in large numbers, and when slavery was abolished by an Act of Parliament of 1833, there was no longer any point in bringing them here at all.

Some black people continued to arrive in Britain: students, sailors, Americans escaping slavery in the USA, and others seeking their fortunes in Britain. These, however, were relatively few in number.

Why did the numbers of black people in Britain not increase naturally as the population as a whole was doing? The answer lies in the fact that throughout the period we have been studying, far more black men came to live in Britain than did black women. For this

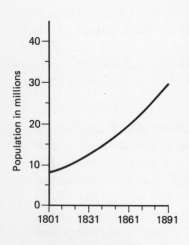

How the population of England and Wales increased during the years 1801–1891

46

reason, many black men married and had children by white women. Many of these children in turn married white people and so on, until the number of truly black people in Britain became very small.

As the numbers of black people in Britain decreased, the once strong black communities in places such as the East End of London, declined, making it more and more difficult for them to help and support their members as they had done in the past. They would also have found it increasingly difficult to organise their own social gatherings, making multi-racial parties more common.

Ira Aldridge, one of the most famous black men in nineteenth-century Britain. He came to England from the USA in 1825 and was soon recognised as an outstanding actor. He played leading roles on the London stage, but met with racial prejudice and abuse as well as praise. While appearing in his first London play, he met and married Margaret Gill, a white woman from Yorkshire. They had four children

Lowest 'Life in London'. This cartoon by Cruickshank shows the type of party described here by Pierce Egan in his book Life in London, *1821:* Lascars (Indian seamen), blacks, jack tars (sailors), and heavers, dustmen, women of colour, old and young, and a sprinkling of . . . once fine girls . . . were all jigging together

Questions

1 Why, do you think, did more black men than black women come to live in Britain during this period?
2 Do you think that life became more or less difficult, for black people in Britain during the nineteenth century? Consider the effects of:
  (i)   The abolition of slavery
  (ii) The decrease in the number of black people in Britain
  (iii) The decline of the black communities
3 Why do you think that so few history books mention the existence of black people in Britain between 1650 and 1850?

INDEX